Chatty Cathy dolls

identification and value guide

Kathy & Don Lewis

COLLECTOR BOOKS

A Division of Schroeder Publishing Co., Inc.

Searching for a Publisher?

We are always looking for knowledgeable people considered to be experts within their fields. If you feel that there is a real need for a book on your collectible subject and have a large comprehensive collection, contact us.

COLLECTOR BOOKS
P.O. Box 3009
Paducah, Kentucky 42002-3009

Cover design: Sherry Kraus
Book design: Pamela Shumaker

On cover: standing (l to r)– Singin' Chatty, $85.00; brunette pig-tailed Chatty Cathy, $135.00; Prototype blonde Chatty Cathy, $135.00; auburn Charmin' with glasses and tag, $110.00; sitting – black Chatty Cathy, $650.00 (pageboy hair style); Tiny Chatty Brother, $80.00.

Additional copies of this book may be ordered from:

Collector Books
P.O. Box 3009
Paducah, KY 42002-3009

@$15.95. Add $2.00 for postage and handling.

Copyright: Kathy and Don Lewis, 1994

Printed by IMAGE GRAPHICS, INC., Paducah, Kentucky

Preface

Dolls have always played an important part in history. As man's technical abilities expanded, so did the variety of dolls. Many toy companies (Ideal, Hasbro, MMAX, etc.) experimented with dolls, trying new things like walking, talking, drinking, and wetting.

Leading the pack was Mattel. They had already made a big impression in the market with Barbie, and now it was time for something new. Many books have been written on Barbie, but very little on Chatty Cathy. We hope this book will shed new insight on why Chatty Cathy became the second most popular doll sold.

Her debut was in early March of 1960 at the New York Toy Fair. This wonderful new doll was available in two hair colors, blonde and brunette. She had a short pageboy cut with those famous short bangs of that time period. Her clothes were very short to reveal the undies, another style that was so popular. Her production span lasted five years, with a five year hiatus.

Then in 1969 she was re-introduced. This time she had a smaller body and her face was redesigned. She was not well received in the market place. That was the end of the Chatty Cathy doll.

This book is intended to give the Chatty collector as much information on these wonderful dolls as possible. This book will provide you with many pictures of dolls, clothing, furniture, patterns, and accessories that are still in existence.

Naturally, somewhere out there someone will have something not pictured or mentioned in this book.

Unfortunately, not all initial selling prices were available to the author; therefore, in some instances we were not able to include them in this book.

Acknowledgments

We wish to thank many people for their input into this book. First and foremost we would like to thank our children, Jason and Tanya, for their acceptance of the time we needed to devote to this book, time that could have been spent on playing catch and other activities.

We wish to thank our parents, Ann and John Kinar for all the help they have given us, the encouragement, and help with the children.

The following people were also very instrumental in providing pictures and encouragement: Lisa Eisenstein, editor Chatty Cathy Collectors Club, Robin Devereaux, Mark Mazzetti, Frances Runnells, Andrew Cunningham, Cynthia Matus, and Deborah Wells.

Thank you to Mattel for producing such a wonderful family of dolls.

To my husband - the wind beneath my wings.

Contents

Foreword

I have been a lover of dolls as far back as I can remember, which happens to be age three. My memory brings to mind three dolls named Weiner, Bologna, and Sausage. Why I named them that I will never know, since I did not like meat.

Along came school, and with school came rules. I was not one to follow the teacher's instructions, rather I wanted to play house and sing songs. In a very short period of time, I became very close to the principle, Mr. Gunther. I spent a lot of time in his office doing what I liked to do, talk. Before long he named me Chatty Cathy. I was not aware of a doll with my name, at least not that I can remember. Nonetheless, this name stayed with me for many years.

Although I still have many of my childhood dolls, my original Chatty Cathy is not among them.

While I was still quite young my father asked for my help in repairing our T.V.s and radios. This was quite a challenge for a little girl.

Being interested in how things worked, loving dolls as much as I do, and being nicknamed Chatty Cathy, one can see how I came to be a toy restorer, specializing in talking and mechanical dolls.

The current prices in this book are to be used as a guide only. Prices quoted are prices realized by the authors, members of the Chatty Cathy Collectors Club, and at doll shows. Please take into consideration the prices will vary from region to region. Current prices will follow each item. Prices quoted for Mint-In-Box (MIB) and/or Mint-In-Package (MIP) will be identified below each item.

The average doll in the Chatty family found today is usually mute, and either nude or redressed. The average price is between $35.00 and $70.00.

Chatty Cathy: Popular As Ever

Reproduced with permission from Kathy Lewis and
Doll World, Dec. 1990, House of White Birches
306 East Parr Road
Berne, IN 46711

In early March of 1960, Mattel Toy Makers won the attention of toy buyers worldwide when they introduced the Chatty Cathy doll at New York's prestigious Toy Fair. Though many "talking" dolls had preceded Chatty Cathy, she was the first with the ability to respond with 11 different phrases when the string on the back of her neck was pulled.

Needless to say, sales boomed in the subsequent holiday shopping season, and many a child found Chatty Cathy under the Christmas tree that year. In 1961, Chatty Cathy was still the only doll of her kind, but her family was to increase in size soon. The next year, Mattel introduced Cathy's talking little sister, Chatty Baby. This irresistible toddler said many baby phrases – all prompted by the pull of her string, just like her big sister.

In 1963, Mattel continued its ride on the Chatty wave of success, adding three members to her family. Tiny Chatty Baby and Tiny Chatty Brother, the twins, were introduced along with their big sister, Charmin' Chatty. Like their earlier siblings, all had pull strings which activated their voice boxes. Charmin' Chatty, however, came with changeable records that gave her a much larger "vocabulary."

The last member joined Chatty Cathy's family in 1965. Singin' Chatty was an adorable doll who recited various nursery rhymes when her string was pulled.

1965 was the final year of production for the original Chatty Cathy family. Chatty Cathy, Chatty Baby and the twins, Tiny Chatty Baby and Tiny Chatty Brother, were reintroduced in 1970 with totally new looks and in different sizes. Like many sequels, however, the new designs were not well-received and production quickly ceased altogether.

The original dolls in Chatty Cathy's family were produced in a wide variety of different "looks," incorporating differences in skin color (including the rarer dark or "black" skin color), brown or blue eyes, and many hair colors. These dolls were assembled from parts made in different countries, and some had hard heads while others had soft ones.

The variations in Chatty's finished appearance were many. One doll, for instance, might have blond hair with ponytails, blue side-glancing eyes and a soft head. But another blond doll could very well have short hair, brown eyes looking straight forward and a hard head.

All these variations meant doll lovers could amass dozens of the Chatty family dolls with no two alike. This makes for a very interesting and challenging collecting experience. I have quite a variety of Chatty family dolls and still encounter new combinations!

Who would have thought that 30 years after their introduction, these unique, charming dolls would still be as popular as they were when they first debuted? Chatty Cathy was a favorite of "baby boom" children. Today, many grown-up baby boomers want their children to have dolls from the Chatty family, too. Or, simply wishing to replace the dollls of their childhood, Chatty Cathy is one of their first choices.

Unfortunately, today's collectors are more often encountering Chattys who are in desperate need of repair. After 25-30 years of being played with or stored, most of these dolls no longer talk.

This presents a problem. Talking dolls that preceded the Chatty family had "Mama" voice boxes which are still available today. But the Chatty dolls used a totally different mechanism for talking and replacement parts are not available. Rather than going to the nearest doll supply store for a voice box, Chatty fans must make repairs themselves – or find someone else to make them.

To get at their voice boxes, Chatty and her friends must be totally disassembled. However, even after doing so, one may find that the voice box is beyond repair or that it is further sealed so that it is impossible to get at the moving parts.

Happily, however, despite these challenges, most Chatty Cathy voice boxes can be restored.

As one who repairs and restores Chattys and their voice boxes, I have received a variety of Chattys in various stages of disrepair. Each one presents a unique challenge. Since the various doll components were manufactured in different countries, the dolls conceal different styles of voice boxes. Only when the body is opened can one find out what is enclosed within – and what type of repairs will be needed. And since spare parts are not available, on must make do with what is at hand.

Children loved their Chatty dolls so much that they took them everywhere, including the bathtub. Naturally, these dolls are rusty and coroded inside. Others have large accumulations of dirt, lint and hair.

Some curious youngsters poked holes through the speaker membrane. Or sometimes, as the result of years of loving use by their talkative owners, the dolls' pull strings fray and break.

Any rubber parts were subject to deterioration, and gummy deposits are sometimes found on the records and other moving parts. These are just a few of the problems I have encountered.

Many dolls have arrived at my shop with notes pleading "Help!" These poor Chattys had been taken apart by someone who was attempting to make repairs, but then hit a dead end once the voice box was exposed. Chatty bodies have arrived in pieces – and I mean pieces! But with time and patience, even these can be "helped," and most – though not all – live to talk to their adoring owners again.

The family of Chatty Cathy dolls are unique, and today's children love them as much as their mothers did. In fact, many of today's buyers of the Chatty Cathy dolls are grandmothers who remember their own children having a Chatty Cathy doll and now want one for themselves. They feel, as I do, that there is nothing better than having a Chatty Cathy doll in one's collection – especially if she still talks to you once in a while!

Chatty Cathy
Body Markings Year-By-Year

The first issue Chatty Cathy body had no mark. This was the prototype doll and was manufactured in 1959. She was first sold in 1960. Her skin color was darker than the later dolls and her limbs had a thicker look to them. Her speaker grill was covered with a tan circular piece of cloth. She was available as either a blonde or a brunette, both had short pageboy hair styles, freckles, protruding tummies, knobby knees, and two buck teeth. Her head was soft.

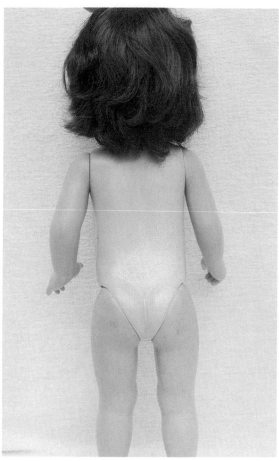

Authors' collection

In 1960 Mattel added a body mark. This was the second issue Chatty Cathy. Within a rectangle on her back it stated, CHATTY CATHY PATENTS PENDING *MCMLX BY MATTEL, INC. HAWTHORNE, CALIF. Beneath this was the Mattel Toymakers, Inc. insignia. It was a circle with their little boy sitting on the letter "M". Her limbs were a little lighter, her head was still soft, and the hair colors were the same. Notice doll below (worth MIB $250.00) still has tan piece of cloth covering the speaker grill.

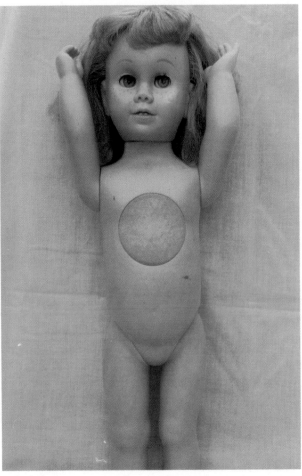

Authors' collection

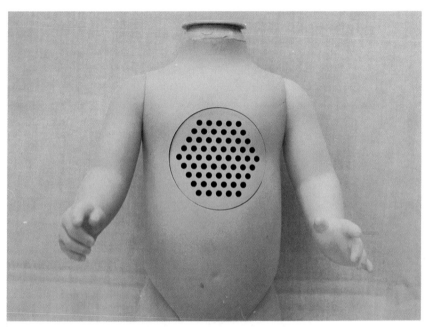

Authors' collection

Next came the open speaker grill with an indentation circling the grill. This was the third issue Chatty Cathy. It has been said that at one time the cloth was there; however, with all of the dolls that we have repaired we have not found one to substantiate this claim. Her body marking read, CHATTY CATHY *1960 CHATTY BABY *1961 BY MATTEL, INC U.S. PAT, 3 017,187 OTHER U.S. & FOREIGN PATS. PEND. The Mattel insignia with the little boy was still there. Her head was still soft, the limbs were the same, and the hair color was still blonde or brunette. MIB $225.00.

This doll along with the others that preceded her said 11 phrases.

Mattel then changed the design of the mechanism. The body now had an open speaker grill with no cloth or circular indentation. This was the fourth issue Chatty Cathy. There was a hexagon pattern of holes around the speaker. This Chatty Cathy model is commonly referred to as the "transitional CC." The head was either soft or hard. The available hair color was now blonde, brunette, or auburn. Some people refer to the auburn as red.

At this time Mattel introduced the pigtail hair style. The body marking varied, CHATTY CATHY PATENTS PENDING *MCMLX BY MATTEL, INC. HAWTHORNE, CALIF. (1960), or the marking for the 1960-61 with the added Other U.S. & Foreign Pats. Pend. with the little insignia below.

It appears that Mattel combined existing bodies and heads with the updated bodies and heads until the old stock was depleted. This is based upon our experience through the many years of repairing these dolls. In time the limbs faded giving the doll a ghostly look. MIB $150.00.

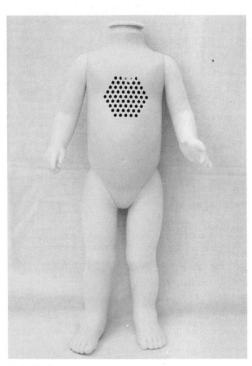

Authors' collection

All Chatty Cathys made from 1959 through mid-1962 said 11 phrases, which included, "I love you," and "Please carry me." From mid-1962 through the end of the original production period, the dolls said 18 phrases, which included, "Let's have a party," and "Let's play school."

The final body marking came in late 1962 and was used through 1964. This was the fifth and final issue in this series. This read, CHATTY CATHY *1960 CHATTY BABY *1961 BY MATTEL, INC. U.S. PAT. 3,017,187 OTHER U.S. & FOREIGN PATS. PEND. PAT'D IN CANADA 1962. This doll had a hard head and pinker limbs. Her speaker grill consisted of a hexagon pattern of holes with an additional four holes beneath it. Her hair style choices were short, long, or the pigtail style. This is recognized by a part sewn down the back of her head to be styled in pigtails. MIB $175.00.

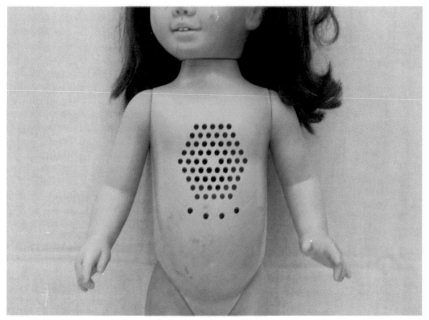

Authors' collection

Pictured here are two blonde Chatty Cathy dolls. The one on the left is a blonde while the and on the right is a strawberry blonde. The one on the right has a definite difference in hair color. This picture does not show the difference too well; however, when one sees it in person they will immediately recognize it as a strawberry blonde.

A special note must be made in reference to the two types of hand configurations found on Chatty Cathy. In one version she has all of her fingers on her right hand open and the other version she is pointing her index finger. Our catalogs show the pointing finger hand in 1960, 1961, & 1962. In 1963 they picture her with both hand versions. Since we have found both styles on dolls from the prototype to the end-of-production models we can not say when the hand style was changed or added. Pictured in the fold-out booklet found with the outfits available in 1961 one will see both hand versions. One thing we are sure of — the ratio of pointing finger to open hand is at least 5-1.

Authors' collection

Clothing

When Mattel first introduced Chatty Cathy, she wore one of two different outfits; either a two-piece sunsuit outfit or a blue party dress.

The two-piece sunsuit outfit consisted of a red sunsuit under a red sundress with white flocked voile attached. The shoulder straps were of the same voile material as was the sash that tied in back. Red velvet shoes with a circle of white pearls and a small bow adorning the top, and white socks completed the outfit. Panties were not included as the sunsuit was the panty.

The doll also wore a red velvet headband with a snap in the back. The Chatty Cathy wearing this dress was stock #682 and sold for $18.00. This particular doll with this stock number was sold for only one year. The outfit was never sold separately. MIB $250.00.

Courtesy of Andrew Cunningham

Authors' collection

Notice the two different fabrics used to complete the sunsuit dress. The one on the left is longer, has a wider sash, and the flocking has more detail than the one on the right. Both are original.

Courtesy of Mark Mazzetti

The other doll available the first year was stock #681. This outfit is a two tone sundress. This dress has a light blue bottom skirt with a darker blue bodice, a white eyelet bolero, panties, petticoat, white cotton socks, and blue velvet shoes. She also has a matching satin hair ribbon with flowers. This was referred to as the Party Dress and was stock #681. Both of these dolls came in a suitcase type carrying case-box with handle.

Notice the different netting and lace used to make the slip. Clockwise: very small netting with closed pattern of lace; small netting with a six hole flower pattern of lace, no holes under flower; small netting with five hole flower and holes under flowers; large netting with three hole flower and no holes under flower. All four of these slips are original. One could have any one of these slips on their doll if it was dressed in the two tone or solid blue party dress.

Authors' collection

Pictured here are two original boleros. The one on the top has the same six hole flower lace as the sleeves and top. The one on the bottom has no flower holes on the sleeves or collar. Both were sold with the two tone or solid blue party dress.

Authors' collection

A colorful eight page storybook, warranty card, and shoehorn were included with a doll. Today these three items are extremely sought after, with the shoe-horn being the rarest. This doll sold for $18.00. Notice the shoe-horn at the bottom right corner of the storybook.

Both boxes #681 & #682 had a checked pattern. #682 had two tones of pink with a pink cardboard insert, while #681 had pink & white colors with a white cardboard insert. They were stamped with the numbers on the top or bottom of the box. MIB $250.00.

Authors' collection

Courtesy of Lisa Eisenstein

Later in 1960 another dress was added. It was identical to the two tone blue dress except that it was solid blue. Original price $4.00. MIP $50.00.

Here is a exceptionally rare dress. It was the same pattern and included the same pieces as the two previously described outfits with the exception that this one had a white skirt. Very few of these were made.

Courtesy of Frances Runnells

In 1961 her wardrobe increased. Available for purchase was a brunette Chatty Cathy dressed in the Peppermint Stick dress, stock #683 (later changed by Mattel to stock #693). This dress was pink with white vertical pinstripes making up the skirt section and horizontal stripes for the bodice and short sleeves, with a white collar, white panties, white cotton socks, and pink shoes. When you examine the inside hem of the dress you will notice a ¾" wide strip of netting. This same netting was used to trim the panties. A white eyelet over-skirt, commonly referred to as a pinafore or apron, went over the dress.

Authors' collection

A matching hair ribbon finished the outfit. This sold for $18.00. This outfit was also available without the doll and sold for $4.00. MIB $225.00. Outfit MIP #60.00.

A Chatty Cathy coat made and sold through Grant's stores was available only in regions where this chain was located. Notice the buttons. They were white with a blue anchor in the middle. I purchased a Chatty wearing the red coat from an owner who had purchased the coat at the same time and store as the doll. Price was $1.29.

Courtesy of Melanie Bowyer

Authors' collection

In this photo you will notice two different widths of stripes. The one on the left is not only wider but longer. It is believed to have been sold on the Canadian Chatty Cathy. We have repaired many Canadian Chatty Cathy dolls wearing this dress.

Nursery School, stock #695, was a buttercup yellow dress with one blue and one red stripe across the bodice. A red pleat insert went down the front. Red velvet shoes, red panties, and white socks completed the outfit. This sold for $3.00. MIP $60.00.

Courtesy of Lisa Eisenstein

Courtesy of Lisa Eisenstein

Party Coat, stock #696, was a red velvet coat with white fur collar with fox-tails, a white fur headband with tails and flowers. This sold for $3.50. MIP $60.00.

Courtesy of Lisa Eisenstein

Playtime, stock #697, consisted of blue denim shorts, white tee shirt, red and white stripe sleeveless jacket, red sun visor, and white sandal type shoes. This sold for $3.00. MIP $60.00.

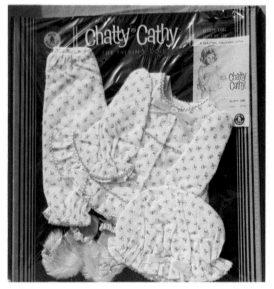

SleepyTime, stock #694, was an adorable pajama set which included a pink and white print bottom, top, and night cap. Furry slipper scuffs completed this outfit. It sold for $3.50. MIP $55.00.

Courtesy of Lisa Eisenstein

Another Party Dress was available with stock number 681. It consisted of a blue and white gingham dress with a collar similar in design to the Peppermint Stick dress. It also had an over-skirt or pinafore-apron. This one had blue velvet shoes and matching hair ribbon. This sold for $4.00. MIP $70.00.

Courtesy of Lisa Eisenstein

Courtesy of Lisa Eisenstein

In 1961 another Party Dress was available. This one was similar in design to the blue Party Dress found on the first Chatty Cathy. This had a solid red bodice, red and white vertical pinstripes, white eyelet bolero, petticoat with red ribbon and eyelet trim, white socks and panties, and red velvet shoes. A matching red hair ribbon with flowers completed this outfit. Stock #693, it sold for $4.00. Note: This outfit was known as the red Peppermint Stick dress and the Candy Stripe dress. Documents showing both names accompanied the dress. MIP $75.00.

Courtesy of Lisa Eisenstein

Chatty Cathy had more outfits to choose from in 1963. Along with the already available outfits, a lucky child could also buy Sunny Day, stock #398, which was a capri set that included a rust, green, and blue sleeveless blouse with a seal and ball applique on the front, rust pedal-pusher pants, rust, blue, and green hat, and blue sandals. This sold for $4.00. MIP $70.00.

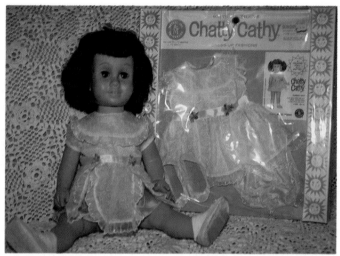

Courtesy of Lisa Eisenstein

Sunday Visit, stock #399, was a beautiful sheer shell pink nylon ruffled dress over deeper pink taffeta, pink satin ribbon sash with pink embroidered flowers attached at the waist, pink taffeta panties, white socks, and pink shoes. This sold for $3.75. MIP $70.00.

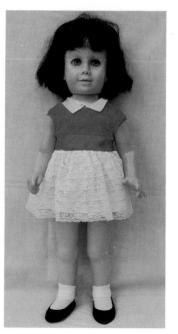

Author's collection

Another dress commonly referred to as a Party Dress, but which in reality had no known name, was a red velvet and white lace dress with red ribbon sash that tied in back. The lace skirt was over white taffeta. White socks, panties, and red velvet shoes completed this outfit. This outfit is not known to have been sold separately. One could purchase a Chatty Cathy, stock #746, wearing this dress, selling for $16.00, or the gift set, stock #396, which included a doll, the above mentioned outfit along with the Party Coat set, and the Sunny Day set which sold for $20.00. MIP $225.00. Note: The black shoes were made for Chatty Cathy but did not come with this outfit.

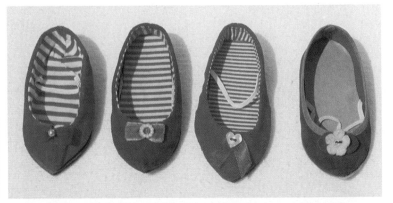

Courtesy of Frances Runnells

In this picture you will see four different Chatty Cathy shoes. From left to right is the order of production. 1) The one on the left has a pearl adorning a bow. The inside of the shoe has very wide red and white stripes. 2) Next came a ring of pearls adorning the bow. Notice the narrower red and white stripes. 3) Then came the heart button adorning the bow with even smaller red and white stripes. 4) Last came the flower on the bow with trim around the top rim of the shoe. Unlike the other red shoes that have a cork or leatherette sole, this pair has a cardboard sole. The inside of this shoe has no stripes.

Authors' collection

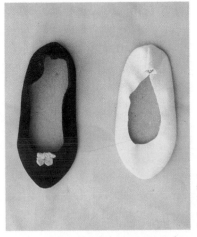

Authors' collection

In this picture you can see a pair of dark blue shoes. These came with the blue jumper dress. When purchasing this dress, one could get either dark blue shoes or turquoise shoes.

Possibly made by Tootsie Toys, producer of many outfits for Mattel's Liddle Kiddle line. Shoes are made of a thin suede material with a cardboard bottom. The black shoe has a flower never seen on the white shoe.

The pink shoes that belonged with the pink Peppermint Stick outfit were the only pink velvet shoes made (see photo, p. 20).

Sunday Visit had a pink taffeta pair but these were distinctly different to from the Peppermint Stick shoes (see top photo, p.25)

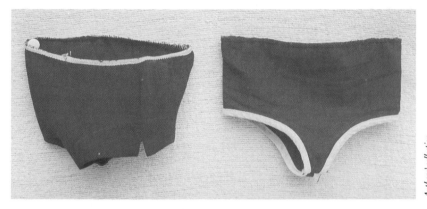

Authors' collection

In this picture you can see the difference between the Chatty Cathy red Nursery School panties and the panties that belonged to Singin' Chatty. Chatty Cathy's red panties had a "v" cut into the side of the leg, whereas Singin' Chatty panties did not. Singin' Chatty panties had a white trim around the legs.

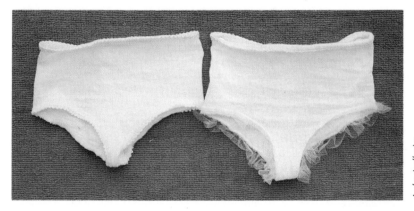

Authors' collection

The main color for Chatty Cathy's panties was white. There were two different styles for the white panties. The pair with the lace trimming the legs belonged to most of the outfits. The pair that belonged to the Peppermint Stick and the blue & white gingham outfits had a net trim around the leg. This trim matched the netting in the underside of the hem of the dress.

These are the only outfits known to the author.

The Chatty Cathy Hair Color Assortment, stock #393, selling to merchants for $96.00 contained the following:

2 each, stock #746 blonde Chatty Cathy in red velvet and white lace dress.
2 each, stock #747, brunette Chatty Cathy in red velvet and white lace dress.
2 each, stock #745, auburn Chatty Cathy in red velvet and white lace dress.

In 1963 Chatty Cathy was available for adoption in the following costumes: (We are sorry photos are not available.)

Auburn Chatty Cathy wearing the Basic Blue costume, stock #745, sold for $16.00.
Blonde Chatty Cathy in SleepyTime Set, stock #824, sold for $15.25.
Brunette Chatty Cathy in Nursery School Set, stock #825, sold for $15.00.
Blonde Chatty Cathy in PlayTime Set, stock #827, sold for $15.00.
Auburn Chatty Cathy in Sunny Day Set, stock #828, sold for $14.75.
Brunette Chatty Cathy in Sunday Visit Set, stock #829, sold for $16.00.

The preceding dolls were purchased through the merchant line, stock #391 and sold for $92.00. This assortment was named Chatty Cathy Dressed Doll Assortment.

Isn't it funny how things turn out? One of the most sought-after outfits and hair colors sold for the least amount of money!

To our knowledge all of the above dolls were sold in boxes picturing Chatty Cathy wearing either the Peppermint Stick outfit or the red velvet and white lace outfit. Only the stock number denoted the doll and outfit inside.

Stock #392, selling to the merchant for $35.50 contained the following:

2 each, stock #398, Sunny Day
2 each, stock #399, Sunday Visit
2 each, stock #694, Sleepytime
2 each, stock #695, Nursery School
2 each, stock #696, Party Coat
2 each, stock #697, PlayTime
1 display stand. This stand is similar to the Charmin' Chatty display stand pictured on page 115.

The Chatty Cathy Master Assortment, stock #394, selling for $171.50, contained the following:

6 each, Chatty Cathy dolls with assorted hair colors
2 each, the Chatty Cathy gift sets
12 each, assorted dress-up fashions
This group was advertised as the "New Look" Chatty Cathy dolls.

What a Christmas treasure to find under the tree! A Chatty Cathy Gift Set! This wonderful set included a Chatty Cathy in any one of the three hair colors dressed in the complete red velvet and lace dress, with the Party Coat Set and the Sunny Day Set. This sold for $20.00 and is almost impossible to find today. We are very sorry that we can not supply you with a photo. MIB $200.00+.

Patterns

A real treat for the little one was the availability of patterns whereby she or her mother could make her own clothes for Chatty Cathy. Advance made two different Sew-Easy patterns for Chatty Cathy. Each package contained four different outfits. Group F contained a pleated skirt and blouse, a sports set, a dress, and a nightgown. Group G contained a coat and hat, rick-rack trimmed dress, pajamas, and a robe. Each package sold for $.75. MIP $12.50.

McCall's made two pattern packages. These were #6465 and #7181. #6465 included a playsuit, pajamas, party dress & panties, dress & kerchief & panties, coat & hat. This sold for $.50 in the U.S. and $.60 in Canada, and was made in 1962. #7181 included a coat & hat, smock, tights, dress, blouse & kerchief, robe, and nightgown. This sold for $.75 in the U.S. and $.85 in Canada, and was made in 1963. MIP $12.50.

Other patterns were available to fit Chatty Cathy. Simplicity, as well as others, made patterns for 20½" dolls. These fit Chatty Cathy. Note: Her name may be on the front or the back of the package. MIP $12.50.

There may have been other patterns for Chatty Cathy; however, these are the only ones known to the author.

Accessories

In late 1962 Mattel gave Chatty Cathy some wonderful playthings. Chatty Cathy cut-outs were now available. Little girls could now take their Chatty Cathy wherever they went.

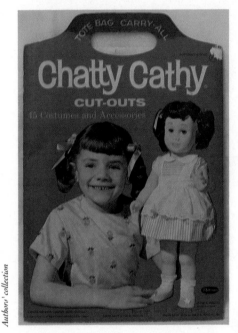

One package was sold in a blue tote bag carry-all. It included 45 costumes and accessories. It was one of my favorites. This sold for $.29. MIP $45.00.

Another set of cut-outs came in a book form and pictured Chatty Cathy on a swing. The price was $.29. MIP $40.00.

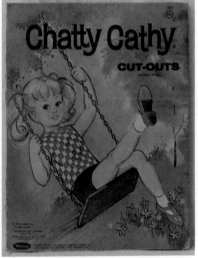

Courtesy of Frances Runnells

Chatty Cathy had her very own armoire (wardrobe). This beautiful piece of furniture was made of sturdy white plastic. The right half had a large door with her picture on it. Inside was a retractable rod with three hangers. On the inside of the door were two racks for her shoes. On the left side were four drawers for her other pieces of clothing. Stock number and original selling price are unknown. $45.00.

Courtesy of Frances Runnells

To match her armoire Chatty Cathy had her very own pencil-point bed. This four poster beauty was made of the same plastic as her armoire, another valued piece of furniture. Stock number and original selling price are unknown. $65.00.

Courtesy of Ruth Kibbons

Courtesy of Ruth Kibbons

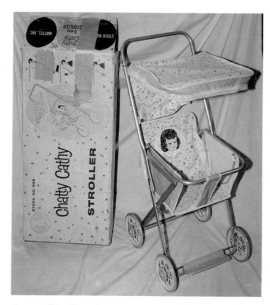

Courtesy of Lisa Eisenstein

Chatty Cathy now had her own stroller. It was a five way stroller which converted into a car seat, backward facing stroller, carry-all bed, sleeper, and regular stroller. This was stock #358, original price unknown. MIB $100.00.

Courtesy of Lisa Eisenstein

Another stroller available was the Chatty Walk 'n Talk stroller. This one featured a strap loop which, when put through the Chatty ring and pulled, would make Chatty talk to you. This pictured both Chatty Cathy and Chatty Baby on the back of the seat. Chatty Baby will be discussed later in the book. This was stock #360, original price unknown. MIB $100.00.

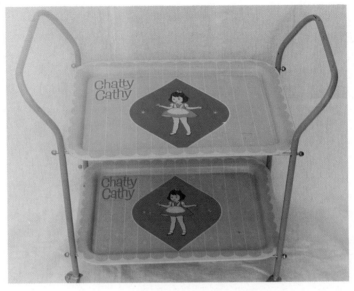

Authors' collection

A little girl could now serve tea to her friends while using her own Chatty Cathy tea cart. This was made of gray steel tubing with two trays picturing Chatty Cathy wearing an apron and little maid's hat. Original price unknown. $50.00.

Courtesy of Andrew Cunningham

While a young mother watched her favorite Sunday Funnies she could also eat her breakfast off a Chatty Cathy TV tray. Original selling price and stock number are unknown. $30.00.

Chatty Cathy dishes were also available. Since I have not seen a complete set I am not able to give a complete description. Pictured here are two plates picturing Chatty Cathy. Original price is unknown to author. $15.00 per plate.

Courtesy of Robin Devereaux

After a very tiring day of playing Mommy the young mother could go off to dream land with her Chatty Cathy bedspread and sheets. Curtains are said to have been available; however, a picture is not available. Stock number and original selling price are unknown. $90.00.

Courtesy of Robin Devereaux

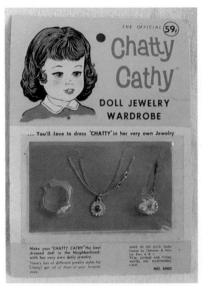

How pretty Chatty Cathy looked wearing her very own jewelry. This set included a hairpin with ruby stone set in a flower on the end, a necklace with a flower charm adorned with a ruby, and a beautiful bracelet with a ruby set into the center of a flower. Original price $.59. $75.00.

Here is another set of Chatty Cathy jewelry. The pieces are the same as the set previously mentioned. The difference here is that the stone in this set is an emerald instead of a ruby.

Theriault's made a jigsaw puzzle featuring many popular dolls of the 50's and 60's. This was titled, "Modern Beauties & Mad Characters" and contained over 500 pieces. Notice Chatty Cathy standing almost in the center. Original price in unknown. $45.00.

Chatty Cathy _____

The following pages are pictures of the various Chatty Cathy boxes. The first boxes produced are known as the pink cartoon boxes. These show Chatty Cathy wearing various outfits and some of the phrases she said. They opened like a book and had a carrying handle similar to a suitcase. At this point, please refer to photo on p. 18. Both boxes are pink check in color. Box stock #682, (one on the left) has two colors of pink with a pink cardboard insert. This doll was wearing the two tone blue dress. Box stock #681, is pink and white check with a white cardboard insert. This doll was wearing the red two piece sunsuit outfit. Both dolls came with an eight page storybook, warranty card, and shoe-horn. All three of these pieces are very sought after with the shoe-horn being the rarest piece. Box only, $30.00. Production period 1959-1960.

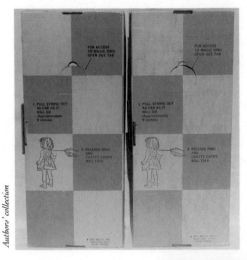

Authors' collection

Here is the back of the production boxes from the first year.

Authors' collection

Here is a close up of color storybook and warranty card.

Authors' collection

The second box was a blue window box that allowed Chatty Cathy to view her prospective adoptive parents.

This photo shows the back of the box. Notice that Mattel changed that also. Box only, $30.00. Production period 1960-1961.

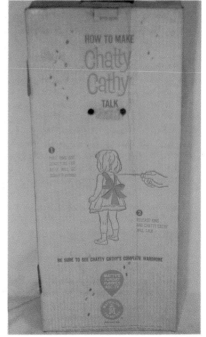

Authors' collection

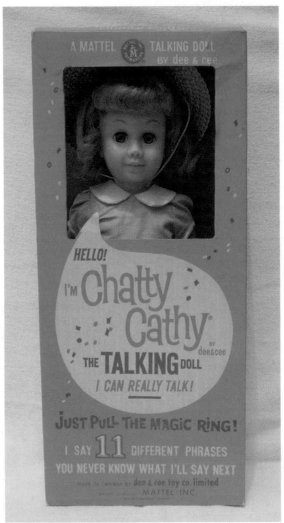

Courtesy of Mark Mazzetti

Here you can see the Canadian version of the blue window box. Notice the dee & cee toy co. limited written across the bottom of the box. Mattel authorized this company to market the doll in Canada. Their dolls had the pinwheel glassine eyes. The skin had a shinier gleam to it. Hat not original.

The third and final box was a picture box that had a picture of Chatty Cathy pasted on the front. Box only, $30.00. Production period 1961-1964.

Courtesy of Mark Mazzetti

All final production boxes pictured the same hair color with the dress being either the Peppermint Stick or the red & white velvet Party Dress. Hair color variation was denoted with a stamp on the box top stating color of hair.

Courtesy of Mark Mazzetti

On the following pages are various Chatty Cathys that we have come upon during our years of restoring these dolls. Many are from our own collection. Because it is hard to say no to someone who is also a Chatty lover, many of the following dolls have found new homes.

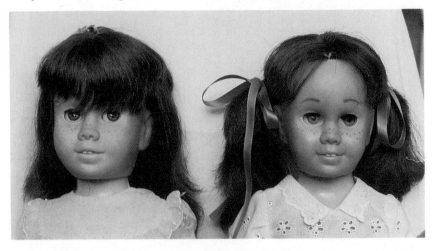

Authors' collection

In this picture you will see two auburn hair Chatty Cathys. The one on the left is wearing her hair down. Notice the different size heads. The one on the left is a soft head. She was made in mid-1962. The other was made in later 1962-1964. Her head is smaller. Both have bangs. The later one, through years of storage, has her bangs parted on the side.

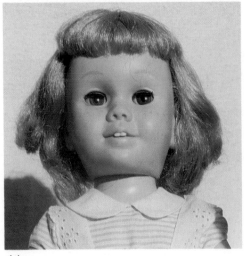

Here is a blonde Chatty Cathy with uncommon eyes; they are a shade of green/gray.

Authors' collection

Mattel made several talking dolls who spoke in a foreign language, but there is no documentation regarding the production of a Spanish speaking Chatty Cathy. This Canadian Chatty Cathy had a Spanish record in her. Some of her phrases were similar to the English speaking Chatty Cathy, slight changes in wording were made. Since our discovery was made public we have heard of only one other Spanish speaking Chatty Cathy.

The engraving on the record identifies it as "Spanish Cathy," whereas the other records read "CC," or "Chatty Cathy."

This beautiful Chatty Cathy was made in Canada by dee & cee toy company, Mattel, Inc. Notice the shine on her face. Her skin was made from a different plastic than the dolls made in the U.S. She is wearing the Sunny Day outfit complete down to the shoes. She has brunette hair and amber eyes. Her eyes have a pinwheel design and are not the standard decal eyes. This doll is very rare.

Authors' collection

Authors' collection

Here is another picture of the soft head auburn pigtail Chatty Cathy wearing the complete Sunday Visit. Isn't she beautiful!

Here is a pigtail Chatty Cathy head made in Canada. Notice the hair lines. The hair was rooted only around the sides and down the center of the head. The heads made in America had rooted hair over the entire scalp.

Authors' collection

Authors' collection

In this picture you will see a rare Chatty Cathy. The bangs are longer than normal. These reach below her shoulders when pulled straight. Also notice how full and curly her hair is. She is wearing the rare blue Party Dress stock #691.

This is the blue gingham dress with the white eyelet pinafore. Notice the shoes. The one on the left has checked insoles that match the blue gingham dress. The one on the right has stripes and belongs with either the solid or two-tone blue dresses found on the early Chatty Cathy dolls.

Authors' collection

Courtesy of Lisa Eisenstein

Pictured here is a rare pigtailed black Chatty Cathy. The majority of the black Chatty Cathys have the shorter hair style known as the pageboy cut. This one is wearing the complete Sunny Day outfit. MINT $700.00.

Here is a very rare find! A blonde hair brown-eyed Chatty Cathy. Very few of these were made. They have only been seen in the soft head version. Mint $700.00.

Courtesy of Frances Runnells

This wonderful Chatty Cathy has brown eyes trimmed with a dark green. These are glassine eyes, as opposed to the more common decal eyes.

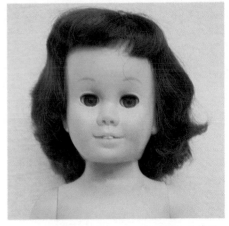

Authors' collection

This Chatty Cathy has eyes in which both the iris and pupil are black. This is the only one of its kind that we have seen or heard about.

Authors' collection

Authors' collection

This unusual auburn Chatty Cathy has brown eyes. Few were made, as we have seen only three others; one of which has brown eye lids usually found on the black Chatty dolls.

The next two photos show a Chatty Cathy with Charmin' Chatty's hair. It has three colors and is much more coarse than Chatty Cathy's saran hair. Notice how long and straight it is. There is no center part going down the back of the head allowing it to be styled into pigtails.

Authors' collection

Authors' collection

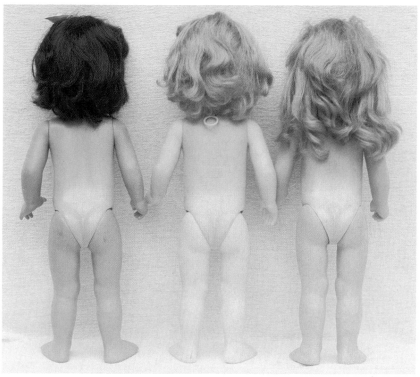

Authors' collection

Finally you will see the three distinct limb colors found on Chatty Cathy dolls. From left to right: early Chatty Cathy with tan limbs, transitional Chatty Cathy with the faded look limbs, and finally the last model with the flesh color limbs. Chatty Cathy varied in size from 19½" - 20½".

NOTE: All three of these babies have morning hair.

In 1980 Mattel authorized Dolls Parts to manufacture a porcelain Chatty Cathy. This doll was made with brunette pigtails and blue eyes. A combination of the blue Party Dresses made up her outfit. There was an eyelet bolero over the blue gingham dress. Blue shoes, white socks, and panties, along with a petticoat, completed her outfit. Dolls Parts added a black pair of tie-up patent leather shoes. Her wrist tag and Certificate of Identity are pictured. Original selling price was $250.00. She was available only through May Co. stores.

We have been told that there were 5,000 made; this doll is number 128. The pin says, "Happy Birthday Chatty Cathy, May Company." This is the store that celebrated her 20th birthday and sold the dolls. On the back of her wrist tag is the store's price tag with their name on it. MIB $700.00.

Authors' collection

Chatty Baby

Chatty Baby was introduced in 1962. She spoke 11 phrases when first on the market and was an immediate success. What little mommy would not want such an adorable little sister for Chatty Cathy? A few of her phrases were "Nice baby," "Cookie all gone," "Doggie bow-wow," and many others.

She was first produced with the Chatty Cathy body that had the ring around the speaker grill. The same body was used for Chatty Cathy and Chatty Baby. The limb openings were different sizes, thus allowing for the different size limbs.

Her early body markings were as follows: CHATTY CATHY 1960, CHATTY BABY 1961, BY MATTEL., INC., U.S. PAT. 3,017,187, OTHER U.S. & FOREIGN PATS. PEND. This particular body has the Mattel insignia underneath the body marking rectangle.

When the second body marking was produced Mattel omitted the Mattel insignia and added the PAT'D IN CANADA 1962. Both body types could have had either a hard head or a soft head. Both blue and brown eyes were available. This doll came with either blonde or brunette hair. Short baby hair was the style.

She was 18 inches tall. Her limbs were shorter and fuller than her bigger sister, Chatty Cathy.

She was sold wearing a removable red pinafore over a lace-edged romper, with red and white slipper socks. She had a pretty red hair ribbon adorning the top of her head. The blonde Chatty Baby was stock #326 and sold for $16.00. (Pictured sitting in the Chatty play table.) MIB $120.00.

Courtesy of Lisa Eisenstein

The brunette Chatty Baby was also wearing the same red pinafore over the white romper, stock #327. She sold for $16.00. MIB $120.00.

Courtesy of Cynthia Matus

Mattel also made a black Chatty Baby wearing the red pinafore over lace romper. Note the original wrist tag, stock #328. She also sold for $16.00. MIB $350.00.

Authors' collection

This picture shows two different panty/slip combos that went with the red pinafore outfit. Remember this was the outfit originally sold on Chatty Baby. Notice the open lace work on the top and the closed lace work on the bottom.

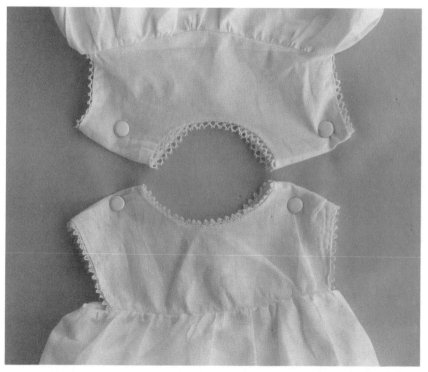

Authors' collection

Clothing

Chatty Baby, like her sister Chatty Cathy, had a complete wardrobe to choose from. The following pages contain the outfits available in 1962.

Playsuit Set, stock #344, was a two-piece terrycloth playsuit with matching booties. The panty had pretty ruffles on the seat. A variation of this outfit had solid booties instead of the striped ones pictured. This sold for $2.50. MIP $30.00.

Authors' collection

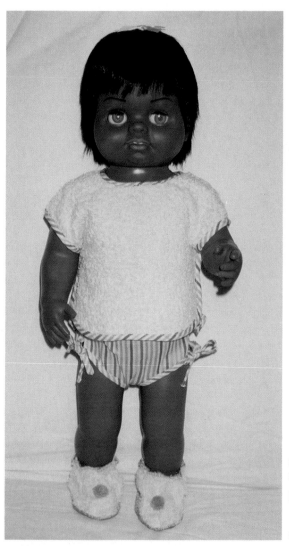

Courtesy of Cynthia Matus

This wonderful rare black Chatty Baby is ready for play in her beautiful Playsuit.

Authors' collection

Sleeper set, stock #342, was a one-piece sleeper with a zipper front and rubber soles. Each sleeper came with a blanket and rattle. The sleepers were sold in two colors, pink, or blue. The blankets varied from solids to stripes. The rattles differed, too. Some were the flat lifesaver type, and others were the round ball type. This sold for $3.50. MIP $40.00.

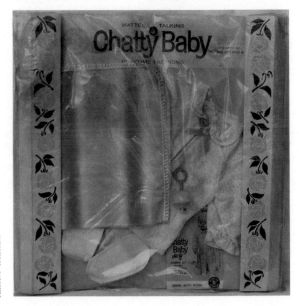

Authors' collection

Here is Chatty Baby in her pink sleeper with her blankie and rattle ready for play before bed.

Courtesy of Cynthia Matus

Courtesy of Lisa Eisenstein

Leotard Set, stock #341, consisted of red leotards with black velvet feet sewn in, white smock top, and white bib with red trim. Chatty Baby was printed in red on the bib. A cute telephone rattle completed this outfit. This sold for $3.50. MIP $40.00.

Courtesy of Cynthia Matus

This adorable Chatty Baby has big beautiful brown eyes
and silky brunette hair. Doesn't she look as if she is
sharing her telephone with you?

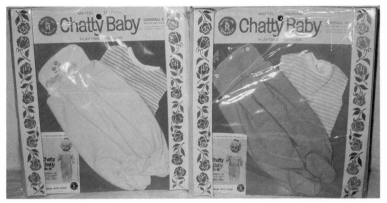

Courtesy of Cynthia Matus

Coverall Set, stock #343, was a nice corduroy-style coverall with sewn in feet; a striped sleeveless tee-shirt completed this outfit. The coverall came in either blue or pink. We have seen both in a light fleece material as well as the corduroy. Both were available with either a pink and white striped shirt or a blue and white striped shirt.

Chatty Baby was printed on the bib portion of the coverall. The writing was in either pink or blue depending on the coverall color; blue coverall having pink writing and pink coverall having blue writing. This sold for $3.00. MIP $40.00.

Authors' collection

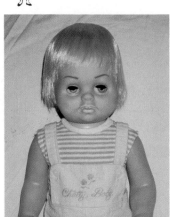

Courtesy of Cynthia Matus

Here is another Chatty Baby showing all of us just how much of a tom-boy she can be. Can't you just see her climbing all over the furniture?

Courtesy of Cynthia Matus

Party Pink, stock #345, was a beautiful pink nylon party dress with cotton panties to match. Pink and white booties completed this outfit. This sold for $2.50. MIP $50.00.

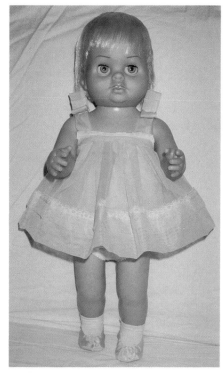

In 1963 Chatty Baby's wardrobe expanded to include two new outfits. Here is Chatty Baby all pretty in her Party Pink. Think she can eat some birthday cake without getting all messy?

Courtesy of Cynthia Matus

Courtesy of Cynthia Matus

Outdoors, stock #348, was a beautiful pink corduroy coat with matching hat. This sold for $2.50. MIP $45.00.

Available for this year one could purchase any of the following dolls: (Pictures are not available.)

Stock #326, blonde Chatty Baby in the red pinafore and white lace-edged romper. This sold for $16.00. MIB $120.00.

Stock #327, brunette Chatty Baby wearing the same red pinafore and white lace-edged romper. This sold for $16.00. MIB $120.00.

Stock #328, black Chatty Baby wearing the same red pinafore and white lace-edged romper. This sold for $16.00. MIB $250.00.

Stock #331, brunette Chatty Baby in Leotard Set. This sold for $15.75. MIB $120.00.

Stock #332, blonde Chatty Baby in Sleeper Set, sold for $15.50. MIB $120.00.

Stock #333, blonde Chatty Baby, in Coverall Set, sold for $15.50. MIB $120.00.

Stock #334, brunette Chatty Baby in the Playsuit, sold for $15.00. MIB $120.00.

Stock #335, blonde Chatty Baby, wearing the Party Pink costume, sold for $15.25. MIB $125.00.

In 1963, the merchants could purchase stock #340, Chatty Baby costume assortment, selling for $31.50 containing:

2 each, stock #341, Leotard Set
2 each, stock #342, Sleeper Set
2 each, stock #343, Coverall Set
2 each, stock #344, Playsuit Set
2 each, stock #345, Party Pink
2 each, stock #348, Outdoors Set
1 display set

Also available to the merchant was stock #322, Chatty Baby dressed doll assortment selling for $93.00, including:

1 each, stock #326, blonde Chatty Baby in basic costume
1 each, stock #331, brunette Chatty Baby in Leotard Set
1 each, stock #332, blonde Chatty Baby in Sleeper Set
1 each, stock #333, blonde Chatty Baby in Coverall Set
1 each, stock #344, brunette Chatty Baby in Playsuit set
1 each, stock #335, blonde Chatty Baby in Party Pink
1 display box similar to Charmin' Chatty's display pictured on page 115

Stock #324, Chatty Baby master assortment selling for $167.50 to the merchant only contained the following:

6 each, Chatty Baby dolls in assorted hair colors
12 each, Chatty Baby assorted dress-up fashion assortment
2 each, Chatty Baby Gift Sets
1 display carton

Stock #323, Chatty Baby hair color assortment, selling to the merchant for $96.00, contained the following:

3 each, stock #326, blonde Chatty Baby in basic outfit
3 each, stock #327, brunette Chatty Baby in basic outfit

Patterns

To our knowledge there were only two patterns made for Chatty Baby. One was made by McCall's and the other made by Simplicity.

Authors' collection

The McCall's pattern #6513, was made in 1962 and sold for $.50 in the U.S. and $.60 in Canada. It did not picture Chatty Baby; however, it had her name printed on the front. It read, BABY AND TODDLER TALKING DOLLS' WARDROBE, also suitable for non-talking dolls. Fits Chatty Baby, Thirstee Cry Baby, Baby Buttercup, Baby Coos, Cream Puff, Betsy Wetsy, Tiny Tears, Pittie Pat, and Baby Toddles. MIP $12.50.

Authors' collection

The other pattern was made by Simplicity, #4839. It did not picture Chatty Baby; however, on the back it named her as one that the patterns will fit. This sold in 1962 for $.45 in the U.S. and $.60 in Canada. MIP $12.50.

Accessories

Lucky Chatty Baby! She had a lot of fun things to play with. The following are pictures of her strollers, playtable, and much more.

In 1962 Chatty Baby shared a stroller with Chatty Cathy. It was the Walk N' Talk stroller. This stroller had a split picture showing both Chatty Cathy and Chatty Baby. Stock #360, the original price is unknown. MIB $100.00.

Courtesy of Cynthia Matus

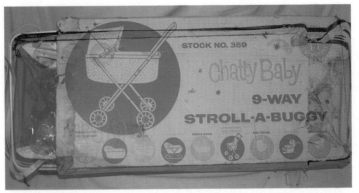

Courtesy of Lisa Eisenstein

Chatty Baby was lucky to have her very own stroller that was much more elaborate than the Walk N' Talk stroller. This Chatty Baby Stroll-A-Buggy converted into nine different playthings. These included a regular front facing stroller, a carry bed, a rocker bed, a swinging bed, backward facing stroller, swing, carseat, a rocker seat, and a carriage buggy. What little mommy wouldn't love all of these pieces in her nursery. Stock #359, original price unknown. $150.00.

Courtesy of Lisa Eisenstein

Chatty Baby Nursery Set included a crib, chair, and wardrobe. Inside the wardrobe there were several hangers, a hanging rod, and a drawer. The wardrobe had two doors. All three pieces were made of sturdy cardboard with wooden legs. A silhouette of Chatty Baby adorned the ends of crib, back of chair, and sides of wardrobe. Stock #318, original selling price was $6.00. MIB $135.00.

Courtesy of Cynthia Matus

Chatty Baby cut-outs were also available. This one shows Chatty Baby sitting down surrounded by many toys. These toys are part of the accessories inside the package. Original selling price was $.59. MIP $30.00.

Another set of Chatty Baby cut-outs that were available came in a sturdy box with Chatty Baby on the cover wearing her outdoors coat and hat. These required no scissors. Original selling price and stock number are unknown. MIB $45.00.

Courtesy of Robin Devereaux

A carrying case was available in either pink or blue. Both picture Chatty Baby on the cover. A "halo" of her phrases are around her. Four of her outfits are also pictured.

Authors' collection

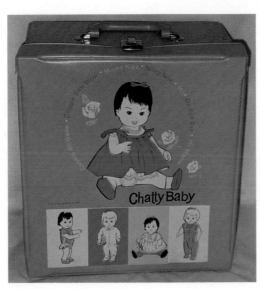

They are the Playsuit, Sleepy Time, Leotard Set, and her Cover-all Set. Inside were several hangers on a rod, a zipper bag, and two pull-out drawers. $30.00.

Courtesy of Lisa Eisenstein

This picture shows the complete inside of the carrying case. It included two cardboard drawers labeled ACCESSORIES. Notice the red and white striped garment bag. This hung on the metal rod attached to the case top. A zipper secured the three hangers inside.

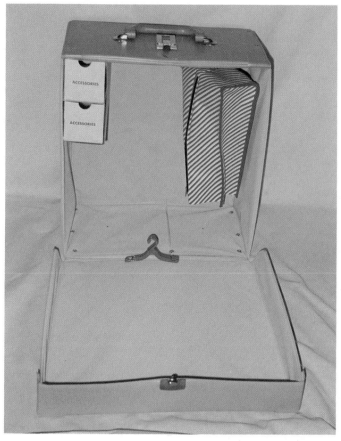

Courtesy of Lisa Eisenstein

Chatty Baby also had two of her own coloring books.

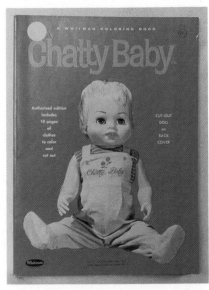

One coloring book had a red cover with Chatty Baby sitting, wearing her pink Coverall Set with the blue striped tee-shirt. Stock #1141, this sold for $.29. $20.00.

Authors' collection

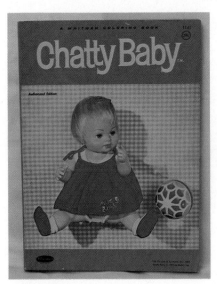

The other known coloring book pictures Chatty Baby sitting, wearing her red pinafore over white romper. The top and bottom borders are red, with pink and white checks in the center. This was also stock #1141, and sold for $.29. $20.00.

Authors' collection

Chatty Baby also had her own Frame-Tray Puzzles. One pictured her standing up wearing her pink romper with the blue striped teeshirt. This was made by Whitman as were most of the paperdolls and coloring books.

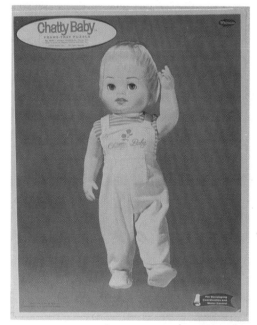

The puzzle had a stamp on the bottom right hand corner which read: For Developing Coordination and Motor Control. Stock #4459, made in 1963. The original selling price is unknown. MIP $25.00.

Authors' collection

Another Frame-Tray Puzzle pictured Chatty Baby sitting while looking at a ball. The background is pink gingham. This also notes, For Developing Coordination and Motor Control. Stock #4459. The original selling price in unknown. MIP $25.00.

Courtesy of Kathleen Smith

Chatty Baby also had her own rocking cradle. This was white and hung suspended from a pedestal stand. Her picture is on the side. Stock number and original selling price is unknown. $60.00.

Courtesy of Cynthia Matus

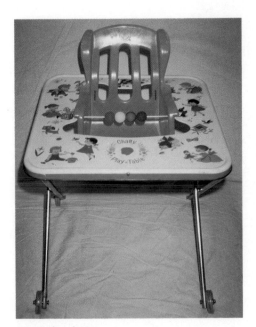

Chatty Baby had a play table all her own. This was versatile as it converted into three different things. The first was a table where she could sit and you could feed her. The second was an adorable rocker. Simply remove the seat and it turned into a wonderful rocker. Lastly, it became a car seat. Simply twist the wire rockers and it now had the ability to hang over the back of the car's seat. Stock #320, sold for $8.00. $50.00.

Courtesy of Cynthia Matus

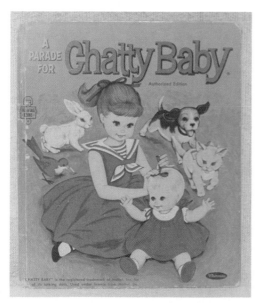

Chatty Baby had her own adventure book written about her titled, *A Parade For Chatty Baby*, by Whitman. This wonderful story book was just the right size for mommy to hold and read to her sleepy baby. Original price $.59. Now $10.00.

Authors' collection

In 1962 Crown Records produced a Christmas album where Santa is sitting surrounded by many toys. In the left corner are two Chatty Baby dolls. One is a blonde and the other a brunette. The whole bottom of the picture looks as if it has been rubbed, where in reality it is fog covering the dolls.

Authors' collection

Chatty Cathy

Here is the back of the Chatty Baby gift set. Included were her Sleeper Set with blanket and rattle, Playsuit Set, Coverall Set, and her Leotard Set. Stock #329 sold for $20.00 MIB $200.00.

Courtesy of Robin Devereaux

Here is a picture of a Chatty Baby box. The only difference between her boxes were hair color. The brunette Chatty Baby box pictured a doll with brunette hair and either blue or brown eyes. The next two pages show the front, back, and cardboard insert of the two different boxes.

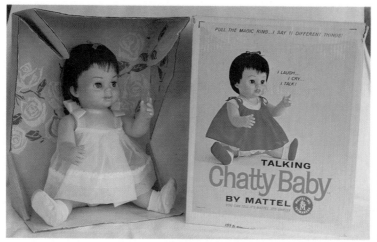

Courtesy of Mark Mazzetti

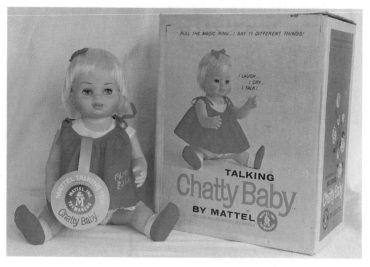

Courtesy of Mark Mazzetti

Courtesy of Lisa Eisenstein

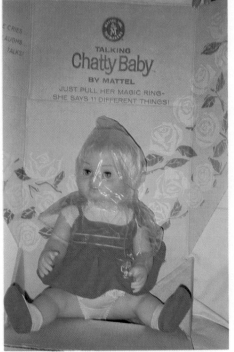

Courtesy of Lisa Eisenstein

What a treasure this satin coverlet is! Can you imagine the beautiful bed the young mommy could make with this?

In 1962 Mattel authorized a company in England by the name of Rose-bud to manufacture their version of Chatty Baby. This doll had hair that was somewhat coarse. Her phrases were the same as the Chatty Baby made in the U.S. She did not have an English accent. Stock # and original price are unknown. $100.00. NOTE: Chatty Baby commonly had one leg shorter than the other, thus she leaned to one side.

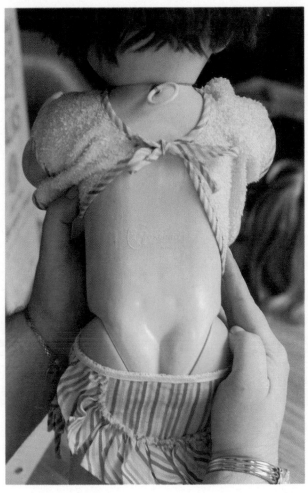

Authors' collection

Tiny Chatty Baby
and Tiny Chatty Brother (twins)

In 1963, Mattel introduced the Chatty Twins. Tiny Chatty Baby and Tiny Chatty Brother were now available. The family was really expanding. Some of Tiny Chatty Baby's phrases were, "Cookie all gone," "Go bye-bye," "Hi Mama," and many others. Tiny Chatty Brother said phrases like, "Go for walk," "Me good boy," and "Hi Mommy," as well as many others.

Many people confuse the two dolls with each other. To our knowledge, Tiny Chatty Brother came only as a blond. We have no record of a brunette Brother ever having been made. Tiny Chatty Brother had a part in his hair located on the right side of his head, Tiny Chatty Baby did not. Quite often one will find Tiny Chatty Brother's romper on Tiny Chatty Baby and they will say that it is a boy. Beware! Look for the side part. It is very distinctive.

Courtesy of Mark Mazzetti

Tiny Chatty Brother wore a boy's style romper with attached shorts. His romper had two buttons on the front. His name was written across his chest. He had a matching cap and booties. Stock #274, sold for $12.00. MIB $150.00.

Tiny Chatty Baby was available with blonde or brunette hair. Her standard outfit consisted of a blue and white romper. The bottom half had blue and white stripes, the top half had an attached white bib with Tiny Chatty Baby printed on the front. White and blue booties and a blue hair bow completed the outfit. Tiny Chatty Baby, blonde hair in standard outfit, stock #270, sold for $12.00. Her original box shows a blonde Tiny Chatty Baby. MIB $120.00.

Courtesy of Andrew Cunningham

Authors' collection

Tiny Chatty Baby, brunette, in standard outfit, stock #271, sold for $12.00. Her original box shows a picture of a brunette Tiny Chatty Baby with brown eyes. MIB $120.00.

Courtesy of Frances Runnells

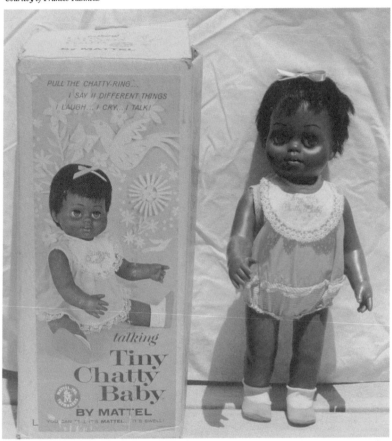

A black Tiny Chatty Baby was available in the standard outfit. Stock #272, this sold for $12.00. MIB $300.00. To our knowledge a black Tiny Chatty Brother was never available.

Clothing

Tiny Chatty Baby had many outfits to choose from.

Bye-Bye, stock #281, was a blue pique coat and matching hat. This sold for $2.25. MIP $45.00.

Courtesy of Lisa Eisenstein

Courtesy of Lisa Eisenstein

Pink Frill, stock #282, was a beautiful party dress made of pink sheer nylon over pink gingham. Panties and slipper-socks completed this outfit. This sold for $2.25. MIP $50.00.

Courtesy of Mark Mazzetti

Fun Time, stock #283, was a coral and pink romper with pussycat embroidery. Hat and booties that tie, completed this outfit. This is one of the harder ones to find. This is also one of my favorites. This sold for $1.75. MIP $50.00.

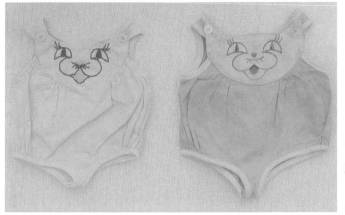

Courtesy of Terry Carter

Here are two variations of the Kitten Romper. One is pale pink with embroidered kitten features while the other is a much darker pink with painted features.

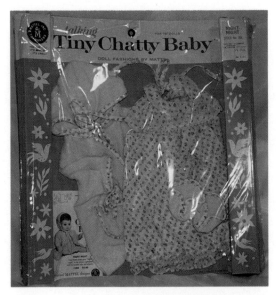

Night-Night, stock #284, was a yellow print nightie with hooded terry cloth robe and slippers. Both gown and robe were full-length. This sold for $3.00. MIP $50.00.

Courtesy of Lisa Eisenstein

Dots-n-Dash, stock # unknown, was a cute dress made of cotton. Bodice was white with red polka dots. A red skirt with a ruffle of white with red polka-dots trimmed the bottom. It had red shoulder straps with a thin strip of white with red polka dots. Matching panties and socks completed the outfit. The original price unknown. MIP $65.00. This outfit is adorable and very hard to find, especially complete.

Courtesy of Mark Mazzetti

The is my all time favorite. This fabulous outfit has no name and is not pictured in any catalog that we have seen. Most people do not know of its existence. It is a beautiful blue gingham sundress bordered with rick-rack. It has a beautiful flowerpot pocket with four red and pink tulips. White tights and tie hightops complete this outfit. Note: The insole of the shoes have the same material as the dress. Stock number and original price unknown. MIB $85.00.

In the picture in the right I have lifted the dress to reveal the tag that proves it is an authentic outfit. Again the shoe is being displayed to show the insole.

Courtesy of Mark Mazetti

Courtesy of Mark Mazzetti

A gift set was available which included Tiny Chatty Baby dressed in her Pink Frill. Two other outfits included were Bye-Bye and Fun Time. Stock #265, this sold for $16.00. MIB $200.00.

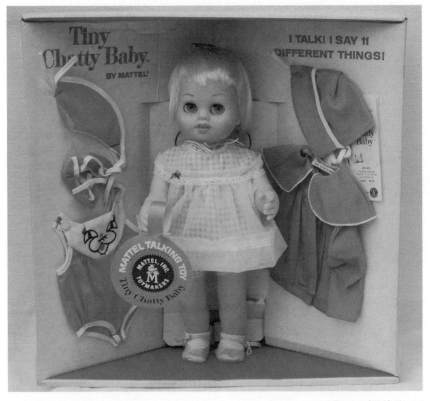

Courtesy of Mark Mazzetti

Update: A call just came in that there is a red Tiny Chatty Baby romper with matching booties. A photo of this was not available to the author; however, the source is very reliable.

The author knows of no other outfits for Tiny Chatty Baby and Tiny Chatty Brother had only one known outfit.

Tiny Chatty Baby was available in the following different costumes in 1963.

Blonde Tiny Chatty Baby in the basic costume, stock #270, sold for $12.00.

Brunette Tiny Chatty Baby, Basic costume, stock #271, sold for $12.00.

Blonde Tiny Chatty Brother, basic (only) costume, stock #274, sold for $12.00.

Blonde Tiny Chatty Baby, wearing Pink Frill, stock #262, sold for $12.00.

Brunette Tiny Chatty Baby wearing Fun Time, stock #263, sold for $11.50.

Brunette Tiny Chatty Baby in Night-Night, stock #264, sold for $12.75.

Once again, the most sought after Tiny Chatty Baby outfit sold for less than any of the other dressed dolls.

The merchant could purchase the Tiny Chatty Baby master assortment for $172.00. This set included the following:

3 each, stock #270
3 each, stock #271
3 each, stock #374
3 each, stock #281
3 each, stock #282
3 each, stock #284
1 each, stock #362
1 each, stock #263
1 each, stock #264
1 window banner

This was stock #278, available in 1963. As with Chatty Cathy and Chatty Baby, we have never found boxes with different pictures representing the dolls in each outfit. Only the stock number stamped on the box denotes the variation.

Tiny Chatty Twins, available together in stock #279-8, sold for $25.00 and consisted of a display holding the Twins while they were riding on a 21" long teeter-toter. Stock #279-3, selling for $25.00 was the same set on the teeter-totter, but without the display.

Stock #280, selling for $27.75 to merchants only was the following assortment:

3 each, stock #281, Bye-Bye

3 each, stock #282, Pink Frill

3 each, stock #283, Fun Time

3 each, stock #284, Night-Night

1 display stand similar to the Charmin' display pictured on page 115

Patterns

To our knowledge there was only one pattern made for Tiny Chatty Baby. This was made by Simplicity, Stock #4839 and consisted of the following: smock, dress, dress and hat, top and pants, pajamas and robe. This was the same pattern made for Chatty Baby with an allowance being made for each doll.

Remember: Chatty Baby is 18" high with a waist of 11½", while Tiny Chatty Baby is 15" high with a waist of 10½". It was made in 1963, and sold for $.50 in US and $.60 in Canada. MIP $12.50.

Accessories

Tiny Chatty Baby had her own satin Cover and Pillow Set. Pink packaging with white pillow and cover inside, trimmed in pink with the name Tiny Chatty Baby printed on them. A pink and blue bow with a picture of Tiny Chatty Baby complete the set. Stock number unknown. MIB $50.00.

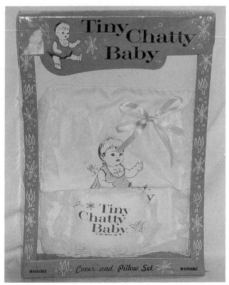

Courtesy of Lisa Eisenstein

While window shopping back east, I came upon this find. A mattress with Tiny Chatty Baby's name and picture on it. How odd! What bed did it go to?

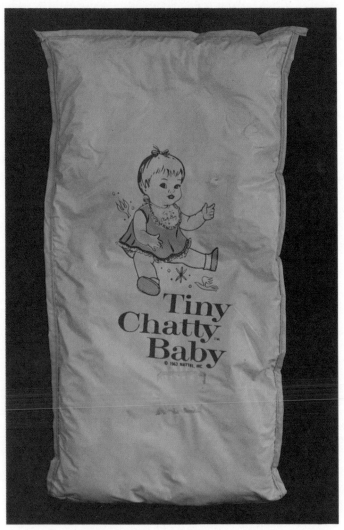

Authors' collection

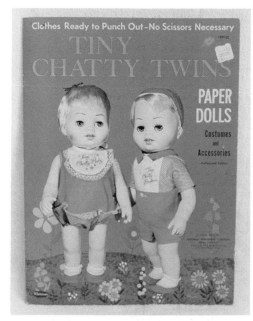

Authors' collection

Tiny Chatty Twins paper dolls were available. This package pictured the Twins standing in a flower bed, and read, "Clothes ready to punch out-no scissors necessary." Stock number unknown, price $.29. These were the only paper dolls for the Twins known to the author. MIP $45.00.

Whitman also made a Frame-Tray Puzzle depicting the Twins on a swing. This one, like the Chatty Baby puzzles, was made for the Development of Coordination and Motor Control. Stock #4464, original selling price unknown. MIP $25.00.

Authors' collection

Mattel did not sell the Twins short in the accessory department either. They, too, had their own coloring book. This wonderful activity book doubled as a coloring book and cut-outs. This activity book is difficult to find. Published by Whitman, it sold for $.59. Mint $35.00.

Courtesy of Lisa Eisenstein

This item features the Twins in their very own Sticker Fun with activity pages. I have never seen this in person. Stock number unknown, it sold for $.29. Mint $45.00.

Courtesy of Lisa Eisenstein

Courtesy of Lisa Eisenstein

Here's an interesting item. It's a Tiny Chatty Baby and Tiny Chatty Brother Color by Number Set. This extraordinary set includes several pictures for the young artist to color. By using eight standard crayons, one could create his or her own beautiful world. Stock number unknown, it sold for $.59. MINT $40.00.

Courtesy of Lisa Eisenstein

Courtesy of Lisa Eisenstein

Tiny Chatty Baby had her own carrying case, too. I have seen it in pink; however, they may have made it in blue also. The right side is clear plastic. Tiny Chatty Baby is much luckier than her sister, Chatty Baby, since she gets to see out of her case. The left side, which is closed, has a rod for hanging her clothes. This was sold only as a set with a doll. Stock number and price unknown. Mint $85.00.

Authors' collection

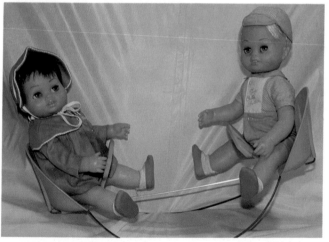

Courtesy of Lisa Eisenstein

One could buy the Twins together on their very own teeter-totter. Aren't they absolutely adorable? I have yet to find one of these for my collection. Stock #2798 sold for $25.00. MIP $150.00.

Tiny Chatty Baby had her own gift set also. This included the Bye-Bye coat and hat set, the Kitten Romper, and Tiny Chatty Baby wearing her beautiful Party Pink outfit. Stock number and price unknown. MIB $225.00.

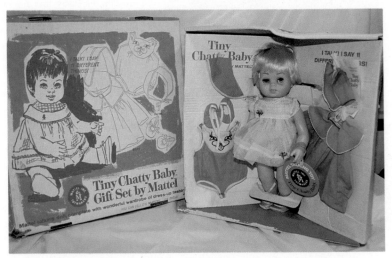

Courtesy of Mark Mazzetti

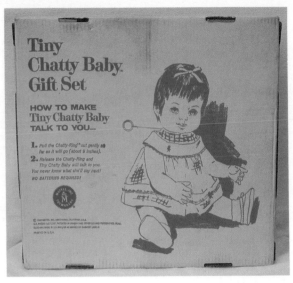

Courtesy of Mark Mazzetti

Courtesy of Frances Runnells

Pictured here is a black Tiny Chatty Baby with her box. She came dressed in the original blue romper and booties. Stock #272 sold for $12.00. MIB $300.00.

A brunette Tiny Chatty Baby adorns the front of this box. Stock #271 sold for $12.00. MIB $175.00.

Authors' collection

These next two pictures show a variation in the Tiny Chatty Brother boxes. In the first picture you will see printed Tiny Chatty Brother with his picture on the front. On the side is printed Tiny Chatty Baby and it reads "You never know what she'll say next. She laughs..cries.. talks!" Standing beside the box is Tiny Chatty Brother holding his wrist tag. Stock number unknown, sold for $12.00. The drawings on the side of the box are of birds and flowers. MIB $200.00.

Courtesy of Mark Mazzetti

Now here is a picture of the Tiny Chatty Brother's box that makes reference to him on all four sides. Notice the boats, cars, and airplanes on the side of the box! MIB $175.00.

Authors' collection

Here is an oddity! A strawberry blonde Tiny Chatty Baby. After repairing and restoring these dolls for four years we have come upon only one Tiny Chatty Baby with this hair color. And the hair is original. None of our catalogs have made any reference to this hair color; only blondes and brunettes are mentioned. Could this mean that there might be a brunette Tiny Chatty Brother out there? If anyone has one, please send in a picture. The two dolls pictured are soft face models. The torso is marked Singin' Chatty; Tiny Chatty Baby; Tiny Chatty Brother. This body marking is not unusual, but the hair is. Tiny Chatty Brother also came in the soft face model.

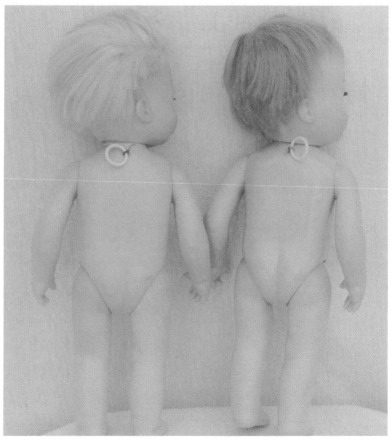

Authors' collection ; strawberry blonde doll courtesy of Sally Rung

Charmin' Chatty

Charmin' Chatty made her debut in 1963. She was 25" tall and looked somewhat gangly, with long, thin, straight legs. She was available in two hair colors blonde and auburn. Glasses made of thin bendable plastic gave her a very intelligent look.

With her came five records which enabled her to say 120 different things. By inserting a record into the side slot, then pulling her string she would talk. Her five records included: Get Acquainted side 1 and 2, Scary Animal Noises, Mother/Ridiculous, Famous/Good, Poems/Proverbs.

Her standard outfit included a pretty navy blue sailor jumper dress that had a white and blue striped middy bib. Her jacket was white with a red sailor collar and a navy blue tie. White panties, red knee socks, and white and blue saddle shoes completed the outfit. The blonde Charmin' Chatty was stock #290. This sold for $20.00. MIB $150.00. This picture shows her in the Travels Set.

Courtesy of Mark Mazzetti

Here is an auburn Charmin' Chatty standing next to her box. Stock #292 MIP $150.00.

Clothing

Eight outfits were made for Charmin' Chatty. Since the back of the boxed outfits are so beautiful we are providing you with those pictures as well.

Let's Play Birthday Party, stock #297, is a beautiful party dress with a red velvet bodice with lace skirt. A red sash tied in the back, white panties and white shoes with red flowers on the top complete the outfit. Included with the outfit are many accessories to have a fun party; party invitations, two party hats, and a cake on a plate with eight candles. This sold for $4.00. MIP $60.00.

Courtesy of Robin Devereau

Courtesy of Robin Devereau

Let's Play Pajama Party, stock #298, is a white print gown, matching slippers, pink curlers, brush, comb, and ribbons. This sold for $3.50. MIP $60.00.

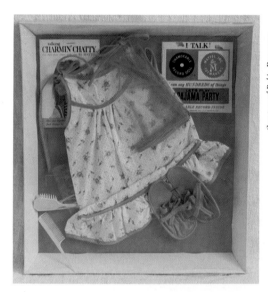

Courtesy of Robin Devereaux

Courtesy of Robin Devereaux

Let's Play Together, stock #299, is a cute outfit with red tights and black plastic shoes sewn in. A red smock with pockets across the front and a matching scarf complete this outfit. This sold for $3.00. MIP $60.00.

Courtesy of Robin Devereaux

Courtesy of Robin Devereaux

Let's Go Shopping, stock #300, is a nice three piece outfit. It has an undershirt that is red with white polka dots over which she wears a blue sleeveless top. It has a border of red rick-rack along the bottom. Her skirt is a matching blue with the same red rick-rack on the bottom. This sold for $3.00. MIP $60.00.

Courtesy of Robin Devereaux

Courtesy of Robin Devereaux

Let's Play Cinderella, stock #362, was a magical outfit for perfect make-believe. This wonderful outfit consisted of a gunny-sack dress with patches, a beautiful pink gown and cape, "glass" slippers that commonly turn an amber color. A broom and magic wand completed the outfit. This sold for $4.00. MIP $65.00.

Courtesy of Robin Devereaux

Courtesy of Robin Devereaux

Let's Play Tea Party, stock #364, gave a little hostess just the right tea set. The outfit included an apron for both Charmin' Chatty and our little hostess, and place settings for two. This sold for $3.00. MIP $65.00.

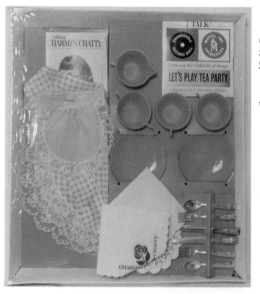

Courtesy of Robin Devereaux

Courtesy of Robin Devereaux

Let's Talk 'N Travel in Foreign Lands, stock #366, this is one of the most sought-after outfits. The set included the following: a stewardess cap with a pin, wings, and flight bag; a red straw hat for Charmin' and a stewardess cap for the little girl, which also had a pin on the side.

Charmin' Chatty had a blue coat, blue shoes, white ankle socks, and white gloves. She was able to carry her own blue stewardess bag along with her red purse.

A language booklet was included as there were an additional four records which enabled her to speak seven different languages. These included, French, German, Spanish, Italian, Russian, Japanese, and English with a British accent. Her passport was also included. This sold for $7.00. MIP $100.00.

Courtesy of Robin Devereaux

Let's Play Nurse, stock #367, included a hospital gown for Charmin' Chatty along with paper slippers. For the little nurse there were accessories that included a nurse's cap, arm band, stethoscope, and hypodermic needle. This sold for $3.00. MIP $65.00.

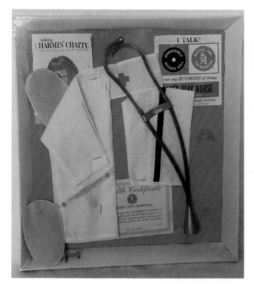

Courtesy of Robin Devereaux

Courtesy of Robin Devereaux

Charmin Chatty Costume assortment was available to the merchant in 1963. This wonderful set included 12 assorted costume sets broken down as follows:

3 each, stock #297, Let's Play Birthday Party
3 each, stock #298, Let's Play Pajama Party
3 each, stock #299, Let's Play Together
3 each, stock #300, Let's Go Shopping
1 counter display

This was stock #287 and sold for $42.00.

Another beauty sold to the merchant was stock #288. this was called Charmin' Chatty Play Set assortment and included the following:

3 each, stock #362, Let's Play Cinderella
3 each, stock #364, Let's Play Tea Party
3 each, stock #366, Let's Talk 'N Travel in Foreign Lands
3 each, stock #367, Let's Play Nurse
1 counter display

This sold for $47.00.

The final merchant deal was stock #294. This contained the following:

3 each, stock #290, blonde Charmin' Chatty in the basic costume
3 each, stock #292, auburn Charmin' Chatty in basic costume
3 each, stock #297, Let's Play Birthday Pary
3 each, stock #298, Let's Play Pajama Party
3 each, stock #362, Let's Play Cinderella
3 each, stock #367, Let's Play Nurse
3 each, stock #498, Chatty Animal Friends & Chatty Animal Round-up Games
3 each, stock #499, Chatty At The Fair & Skate 'N Slide Games

This whole collection sold for $175.50.

Accessories

Charmin' Chatty had two game boxes available. With the insertion of a record one could actually play games with her.

Chatty Animal Friends & Chatty Animal Roundup were in one package. This game box contained two playing boards. Game cards, a spinner, and game pieces to be moved around the board completed the set. Stock #498, this sold for $2.00. MIB $50.00.

Authors' collection

Authors' collection

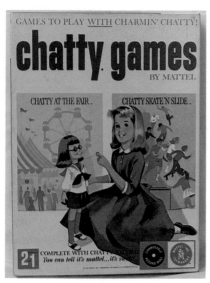

Authors' collection

Chatty At The Fair & Skate 'N Slide were also in one package. Reversible game boards, game pieces, and a spinning wheel made up the package. Stock #499, this sold for $2.00. MIB $50.00.

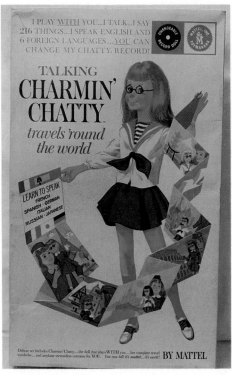

Courtesy of Mark Mazzetti

Charmin' Chatty Travels Around the World gift set is the most sought after gift set. This included the doll in either hair color, dressed in the original sailor suit. Complete travel outfit mentioned earlier, plus records, purses, hats, and booklets were included. Stock #295, this sold for $25.00. MIB $400.00.

Courtesy of Robin Devereaux

Here is a close-up of the elusive passport that seems to be missing from most Travel Sets. It features stamps from many of the countries that Charmin' has visited.

Here is a picture of the translation booklet and passport (opened). Both are very hard to find and a must for the Charmin' die-hards.

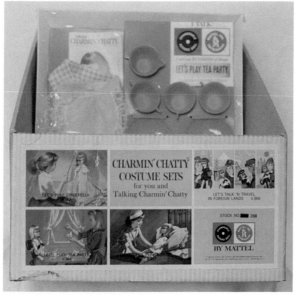

This wonderful display was not meant to be sold. It was the stores' display to hold the Charmin' Chatty outfits. What a treasure to add to one's collection.

Charmin' Chatty also had paper dolls (cut-outs) available. This set shows her wearing six of her eight outfits. Stock #1959, sold for $.29. MIP $45.00.

Authors' collection

Another paper doll set featured her Travels Around the World wardrobe. Stock # 1959, sold for $.39. MIP $45.00.

Authors' collection

Magic stay-on doll and clothes were also available. Stock number unknown, price unknown. MIP $45.00.

Courtesy of Robin Devereaux

This beautiful Charmin' Chatty paper doll activity book included: doll to punch out, story to read, pictures to color, a horse and saddle to punch out, a chuckwagon to assemble, and other things to do. Published by Golden Books. Original price $.29 Mint & Uncut $45.00.

Charmin' Chatty had her own Play Hats as well. This wonderful set had seven hats for Charmin' and seven hats for the little mommy to wear. Simply punch-out the hats and clothes, dress Charmin', put on the girl's hat and you're ready for play. Original price $.29 Mint $50.00.

Authors' collection

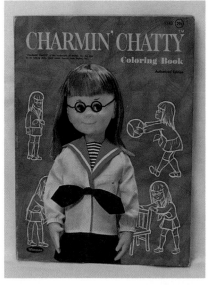

Charmin' Chatty had a coloring book as well. This features her from the waist up. In pencil drawings you can see Charmin' in four different positions. Stock #1143, sold for $.29. MIP $25.00.

Authors' collection

Authors' collection

Charmin' Chatty made it big. She was pictured on the cover of the *Saturday Evening Post*, December 7, 1963 Editions. She was pictured from the waist up holding a bluebird in her left hand. This sold for $.20. Unfortunately, there is no write-up regarding this doll contained in the magazine's text. MIP $45.00.

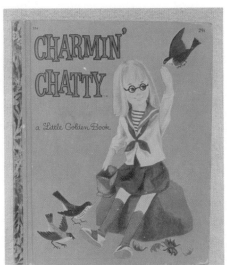

Golden Books also featured Charmin' Chatty. This book pictures Charmin' feeding blue birds while she sits on a rock. Stock #554 this sold for $.29. $15.00.

Authors' collection

Whitman made two puzzles for Charmin' Chatty. The first puzzle shows Charmin' on her way to catch a plane. She is carrying her suitcase and her passport. In the background is an American Astrojets plane. This, like the other Whitman puzzles, was produced to assist youngsters in developing coordination and motor control. Stock #4428, original selling price is unknown. MIP $30.00.

Authors' collection

The second puzzle made shows Charmin' Chatty celebrating her birthday. She is holding her birthday cake. She is wearing her party hat. Behind her are a row of balloons and several gifts. Stock #4457, original selling price is unknown. MIP $30.00.

Authors' collection

Courtesy of Mark Mazzetti

Finally, here is a picture of the box top for the Charmin' Travels 'Round the World box set.

Singin' Chatty

    This delightful doll was made for one year only and was the last of this series. She was available as either a blonde or brunette.

    This Singin' Chatty is a brunette wearing one of the three outfits available. A red dress with music notes, white bow at her waist, white collar, red panties with white trim, white socks, and red plastic shoes completed this particular outfit. Stock number and original selling price are unknown. MIB $125.00.

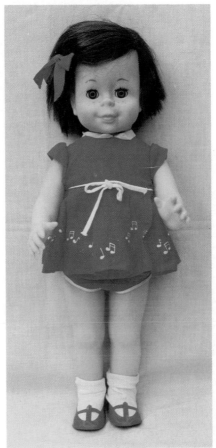

Authors' collection

In this picture we see a blonde wearing the red dress with a white collar and a white bib on which there are two buttons and a red bow. Music notes dance across the bottom of the dress. This doll is pictured with her box. Stock number and original price unknown. MIB $125.00.

Authors' collection

Courtesy of Andrew Cunningham

Here is the back of the Singin' Chatty box. Notice the hole in the box which allows a potential mommy to test her baby before adopting her. I'm sure some mommies today would like to be able to test their babies prior to the commitment, too! Ha! Ha! Ha!

This Singin' Chatty is very rare as she has bangs. Very few were made with straight bangs. She is wearing the same outfit as the blonde in the photo on page 123. Stock # and original selling price are unknown. She also has her wrist tag. MIB $175.00.

Authors' collection

Did you notice the two different dresses Singin' Chatty was wearing? The brunette is wearing a dress with a tie in front and music notes on the bottom. The blonde is wearing a dress with a white bib insert, no tie, and music notes along the bottom.

Now to help clear up the confusion I may have caused, here are three different Singin' Chatty dresses. One could purchase their doll wearing any one of these.

Top left: bib style with music notes and her name across the bottom. What? Another different dress! Now we have seen a total of three dresses. That's right! Three!

The one on the right has the tie and music notes and has pleats in the front, the one on the bottom has the bib and music notes minus the name and is gathered in the front. The shoes are the original ones, as are the panties. Chatty Cathy has a similar pair of panties that go with her Nursery School dress. The difference between these is that Chatty Cathy's panties have no white trim and Chatty Cathy's panties have a "v" cut into the side of the leg; these do not. (See the photo on page 27 in the Chatty Cathy section.)

These dolls say 11 nursery rhymes such as "Ring around the rosy, pocket full of posy," "London bridge is falling down, My fair lady," and "Row, row, row your boat, life is but a dream."

We have neither seen nor heard of any accessories made for Singin' Chatty. Poor dear! Why they would neglect to make more things for her is beyond all of us Chatty die-hards.

Authors' collection

Pictured here is the black Chatty family. From left to right: Chatty Baby, Chatty Cathy (in back), and Tiny Chatty Baby. A black Tiny Chatty Brother was never made as far as our records show.

Authors' collection

Reissue Chatty Cathy and Family

In 1969 Mattel reissued Chatty Cathy. Her phrases had been changed to now include whispers, nursery rhymes, and some of the original Chatty Cathy phrases. She is a cross between Chatty Cathy, Singin' Chatty, and Baby Secret. Stock number and original price are unknown. MIB $50.00.

Authors' collection

Courtesy of Mark Mazzetti

Here is a picture of the reissue Chatty Cathy in her pink box.

Authors' collection

In this photo you can see her in the black version. Stock number and original price are unknown. MIB $75.00.

Courtesy of Mark Mazzetti

In the early 1980's Mattel introduced Chatty Patty. She had painted features similar to the reissue Chatty Cathy. This doll had a hole in her right hand which allowed toys to be inserted. When a toy was inserted and her string pulled she would talk about what she was holding. Stock number unknown. Her original selling price was as low as $10.00. MIB $40.00.

Rosebud in England made a couple of dolls with the Chatty record. These two beautiful dolls are often passed up at doll shows because they are not well known. Any Chatty collector should be proud to have these two dolls in their collection. Their phrases are similar to the dolls made in the U.S., but with British accents. The names of these two dolls are not known by the author nor are the stock numbers or original selling prices. Current price unknown.

Fun Photos

Now let's take a few minutes to enjoy a few days in the life of Chatty Cathy and her family.

Here we see the whole family baking something good.

Here we see Singin' Chatty being taught to color by Chatty Cathy.

Courtesy of Frances Runnells

Courtesy of Frances Runnells

Now Singin' Chatty will play the violin for our enjoyment.

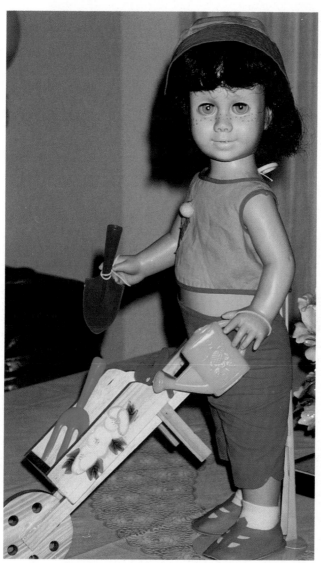

Courtesy of Frances Runnells

Chatty Cathy must tend to her garden so they will have food to eat.

Chatty Cathy is busy baking a surprise for someone.

Courtesy of Frances Runnells

Courtesy of Frances Runnells

Look at how beautiful the cake looks. Want a piece?

Courtesy of Frances Runnells

Let's get tomorrow's clothes ready. What shall I wear?

Courtesy of Frances Runnells

Will I ever get these tangles out? Too much partying, I guess!

Courtesy of Frances Runnells

I sort of burnt the toast. Oh well! The tea is still hot.

Courtesy of Frances Runnells

Chatty Cathy is leaving for a trip. She has her camera in her hand. Where do you think she is going?

Where else would a star like Chatty Cathy go for a vacation! The French Riviera, of course!

Storage and Travel tips for all talking dolls:

Never store in an attic. Heat is very destructive to the voice-box.

Never get the doll wet, this will cause the voice-box to rust.

Always store doll with protection, bugs and dust will enter the body through the speaker grill and cause damage when the string is pulled.

Always store the doll in a dust-free environment, preferably in a display case or cabinet, again, dust will cause damage to the voice-box.

Never store the doll in direct sunlight, this will cause skin damage, eye fading, and possible over-heating of the voice-box.

Avoid cellars or basements, the dampness will cause damage to the doll and voice-box (cloth dolls are easpecially vulnerable to mold and mildew).

Never apply lubricating oil to the eyes, most Chatty eyes are a decal and the oil will ruin the paper.

When traveling, do not forget about your doll when you lock your car or motorhome. Like animals, dolls need a temperature controlled environment.

If you happen to be taking a talking doll on a plane, save yourself a lot of time and hassle by going straight to the security office and declaring your doll. The voice-box has metal parts that when put on the X-ray belt look similar to a handgrenade. By declaring your doll immediately to the proper airport authorities, you will save time and save yourself the heartbreak of having your doll either dismembered or confiscated!

About the Authors

Kathy and Don Lewis live in Thousand Oaks, CA. They have two children, Jason 15 and Tanya 13. They operate a business named Chatty Cathy's Haven where they repair and restore talking dolls and toys. They have been in business for several years and have customers overseas as well as in Canada and in the U.S.

The Chatty Cathy Collectors Club

Since 1989 Lisa Eisenstein of Piscataway, NJ, has edited an extensive newsletter for Chatty fans called the *Chatty News*.

The membership is all over the country and overseas. The newsletters focus on owners of Chatties who share their photos and interesting stories for all to enjoy. For club and newsletter information please send a self-addressed stamped envelope to:

LISA EISENSTEIN
2610 Dover St.
Piscataway, NJ 08854-4437

All inquires must include a SASE for a reply.